Raising Your
Daughter
Through the
Joys, Tears &
HORMONES!

RAISING YOUR DAUGHTER THROUGH THE JOYS, TEARS & HORMONES!

C. LYNN WILLIAMS

Author of Trying To Stay Sane While Raising Your Teen and
The Pampered Prince: Moms Create a GREAT
Relationship With Your Son

220 Publishing

Chicago, Illinois
220 Publishing
(A Division of 220 Communications)

Published by 220 Publishing
(A Division of 220 Communications)
PO Box 8186
Chicago, IL 60680-8186
www.220communications.com
www.twitter.com/220publishing

Cover design and inside layout by Julie M. Holloway
www.jmhcre8ive.com

Library of Congress Cataloging-in-Publication data
Williams, C. Lynn Raising Your Daughter Through the Joys, Tears & HORMONES!/C. Lynn Williams. – First edition
pages cm ISBN 978-1-6284-7448-0. Raising Daughters-Parenting-Women's Nonfiction. 2. Teenagers.

ALSO BY C. LYNN WILLIAMS

TRYING TO STAY SANE WHILE RAISING YOUR TEEN: A Primer for Parents and The Pampered Prince: Moms Create a GREAT Relationship With Your Son

PREFACE

C. Lynn Williams speaks with a refreshing honesty. Her voice provides an interesting perspective on how to effectively improve communication and self-esteem. Her book provides a roadmap for self-discovery that will benefit not only caregivers who are raising daughters, but also those who do not have children, but have been daughters themselves. Even men who find themselves asking why some women are the way they are or are puzzled by how women think will benefit from reading Raising Your Daughter Through the Joys, Tears & HORMONES!

Thank you C. Lynn for adding to this body of knowledge!

- Dr. Melanie Brown, Pediatrician
University of Chicago Comer Children's Hospital

Raising Your Daughters Through the Joys, Tears and HORMONES! is a well-written & practical guide every parent should own to assist them in raising their teenage daughters to become empowered women. This book makes a difference.

- Rev. Courtney Clayton Jenkins, Pastor & Teacher
Euclid Avenue Congregational Church
Cleveland, Ohio

Additional Praise about C. Lynn Williams' Books

Trying to Stay Sane...is a must read! It is thought provoking and gives practical suggestions for difficult situations. I found it useful both with my own children as well as a resource for my patients.

- Traci Powell, MD
Board Certified Psychiatrist

Ms. Williams has hit the nail on the head with her books, *Trying to Stay Sane While Raising Your Teen* and *The Pampered Prince: Moms Create a GREAT Relationship with Your Son*. She has written books that provide tremendously useful tools for learning to successfully understand the needs of children and how to effectively parent them!

- Michelle Hoy-Watkins, Psy.D.
Clinical Forensic Psychologist

CONTENTS

Foreword

FOREWORD

The older I get, the more I promise myself that I will mind my own business. The problem is that I am at that wonderful age that I no longer care what people think, and I feel much better saying what is on my mind! As I was finishing my book, *The Pampered Prince: Moms Create a GREAT Relationship with Your Son*, I began to notice interactions between women and their daughters. Sometimes the interactions were wonderful and heartfelt; other times, I cringed as the mother harshly spoke to her daughter or simply cursed her out and called her a bitch. Not good!

I have written this book to properly address issues that often occur in mother & daughter relationships, and to suggest better ways to manage our daughters as they move from girlhood to the complicated world of adolescence, teenville, and finally into womanhood.

I am thoroughly convinced that loving and nurturing our 'girls' will allow them to make better choices in their lives. They won't feel that they have to conform to the women they see on reality shows, choose men who see them as property as opposed to human beings, become super women, or have children because they just want someone to love them for who they are.

This book is devoted to my mother, my daughters, and mothers and daughters all over the world.

Peace and love,
CLW

"A wonderful, loving secure mother-daughter relationship makes for a secure, confident young woman."

CHAPTER ONE

JUST WHAT IS A PRINCESS ANYWAY?

When I was a little girl, I wanted to be just like my mother. Nobody told her what to do and she wore make-up. She wasn't afraid of anything or anyone, and she helped me defeat the bullies in my life, even if her methods were *Gestapo* in nature.

Ever have your daughter do something that you thought you would seriously get into her for? Sassing you or talking back? Did she talk under her breath or sigh loudly when you asked her to do something as well? "I'm gonna hurt that chile if she rolls her eyes at me one more time..." Ever felt like that about your daughter? Your little princess?

When I was growing up, any of those offenses resulted in stern punishment. Rolling your eyes may have gotten you knocked to the floor too—it wasn't tolerated. There was not a lot of yelling done by old school mothers. If you misbehaved, you got the 'look', a pinch, or a spanking. Grooming and training.

While there are other definitions for 'princess', Webster's Dictionary defines a princess as a female member of a royal family. And everyone knows that a princess, with the proper training, grows into a wonderful and wise queen. But a princess doesn't automatically become a queen—she is groomed and trained.

I never felt like a princess... I wore glasses, played baseball, climbed trees, and scraped my knees often. I was, and still am, an adventurer! I loved reading, playacting, and I marched to a different drummer. I asked embarrassing questions and always wanted to know the reasons why (for most things). This is the material that my mother had to work with. It was her responsibility to take this little outspoken, self-conscious, tomboyish daughter and prepare her for life as a self-confident female able to raise her own family one day.

I waited several years before starting my own family. Even though I was married, I couldn't imagine having children. I wasn't sure I would make a good mother—or that I even liked kids! Waiting to have kids was important to me because as an adolescent and teenager, I babysat—a lot! If I wasn't babysitting my brother and sister, I babysat the kids on the block or wherever I was needed. It was a great way to make money, and as a sheltered girl I had limited going out weekend privileges, so babysitting got me out of the house and I was able to make money as well! The major problem I had with babysitting was that I began to hate kids because of how dependent on you they are. Being responsible for my sister and brother was a big enough responsibility; but having children of my own… that was another story altogether.

From my perspective, the children I babysat were seldom well-behaved: My kid sister was bratty, and I never had alone time because I usually had the responsibility of taking my brother and/or sister with me everywhere I went. By the time I left for college, I'd had enough of young children! These experiences were the best birth control method available, and I highly recommend that you have your daughter(s) babysit for a young couple!

As a young princess, I discovered that all of that time babysitting and care-taking of my siblings gave me excellent managing and coping skills that were useful in my adult life. However, at the age of sixteen or seventeen, thinking about the potential benefits down the line of having younger siblings is not what's on your mind!

Princesses need constant wisdom and guidance. Thankfully, I had a wise mother and group of aunts and grandmothers who helped me grow from a little girl into the 'talented' woman I am today! These women were not afraid to chastise, groom, love, and nurture me.

Meanwhile, I had a love/hate relationship with my mother. I loved her because she was my mom and a great role model. But she was so *strict* that I hated how cold and callous she could be when it came to reprimanding and punishing me. I watched a lot of war movies and thought she was a perfect drill sergeant!

My sister and I were her top priority and she took her job as #1 Mom, very seriously. As her little princess, I watched, admired, and feared my mother. She was a woman of her word. She did what she promised—good or bad. She wasn't demonstrative, so I didn't hear a lot of 'I love yous', but I knew I was loved; and I could count on her. She was factual, critical, and demanding, but I would have liked to have heard the 'I love yous'. As you raise your daughter, it is important for her to understand what you expect of her. However, it is equally important that you both tell and show her how much you love her as well. Many young women get the benefit of their mother's wrath and training without the pleasure of their open love and support. I believe the pure unadulterated love is what is missing from our relationships with our daughters. Is this missing link what pushes our daughters into the arms of abusive boyfriends or early sexual encounters?

Sure, the kind of father/daughter relationship has a lot to do with the kind of man a woman is attracted to; but you better believe a wonderful, loving secure mother/daughter relationship makes for a secure, confident young woman.

As a teen, I felt I could never please Mom. It wasn't something we talked about until I became a parent. But at the time, it was really tough for me because I started to feel that it didn't matter how much I did around the house or at school, she would not be pleased. If I got all 'A's and one 'B', she would say, "Why did you get a B?" If I started dinner, she wanted to know why I didn't also set the table. When I made it home on time, she didn't praise me and say, "Good job, Cheryl." When I took a different bus route home, she wondered why I tried a new way instead of taking a familiar route. After a while, I stopped expecting her praise because it seemed too difficult to earn. Mothers, decide how important the tasks you expect your daughters to achieve are, and not continue to raise the bar in unrealistic ways.

You might like to check out my book, *"Trying to Stay Sane While Raising Your Teen"* to understand my mother's perspective as a parent and mine as a teen.

What are mothers supposed to do with daughters who are impulsive, emotional, and pretty headstrong? Well, talk to them, teach by example, and tell your daughter your story. That's what my mom did for me. She told me things I needed to know: For example, she told me about the birds and the bees as soon as she thought I was ready; she told me how important my virginity was and not to give it away; she gave me permission to attend a local organization's teen Q&A session to ask questions that I may have been afraid to ask her.

Any project that I attempted, she encouraged. I learned to love and appreciate opera because together we listened to the Metropolitan Opera radio broadcasts on Saturdays. Gourmet cooking wasn't her specialty, but she baked cakes and pies from scratch and I helped her. She taught me about being discriminating when it came to my relationships with other people. I remember her saying, "That girl is trouble, stay away from her." I never understood how she could tell me about a friend without really knowing—and yet she was never wrong!

Suffice to say, I learned a lot from my mom. She was the queen and I was the princess. Again, one of the most important jobs of a queen is to groom her princesses into future queens. Princesses who have been well-groomed turn into strong, confident women. They matriculate through their teen years and survive them without succumbing to the 'evils of the world' (premarital sex, teen pregnancy or dropping out of high school just to name a few).

Princesses can stand up for themselves, even when their female counterpoints have different opinions. You know what I'm talking about? For example, you and your girls get together every Friday after work, and you've decided to move to another city to pursue a career interest. Your friends are devastated and try talking you out of it. "I mean, you'll be 2000 miles away and we won't be able to meet weekly. Aren't you afraid?" You tell your girlfriends "No, everything will work out. I'll be fine." The well-groomed princess is excited about the challenge and looks forward to it with confidence.

STUDY GUIDE QUESTIONS FOR JUST WHAT IS A PRINCESS ANYWAY?

1. When you were growing up, did anyone call you a princess? If yes, explain why, where, when.

2. What positive images come to your mind when you think of a princess? Why do think you have these positive associations?

3. What negative images come to your mind when you think of a princess? Why do think you have these negative associations?

4. Are there any reasons preventing you from nurturing your daughter as a princess?

CHAPTER TWO

OH, THE SACRIFICE!

Working with our young girls and turning them into young ladies (princesses) takes a lot of time and sacrifice. Make no mistake, just like a gardener, you will plant, water, and prune daily. Girls aren't born knowing what to do and say. It's your and her father's responsibility to teach those things to them. You teach and show by example, which means your daughter learns about hygiene, good manners, and study habits from you. If I was musty from playing outside, my mom made me wash up. I learned how often to change my sanitary napkins from my mom, not the school nurse. We were taught that leaving the house with rollers in our hair was unthinkable. Who did that? If your hair wasn't 'done' by the time you needed to leave the house, you either didn't leave or you wore a different hairstyle. Wearing house slippers to the grocery store was unheard of in our family. Wearing shorts was permitted on the block, but if you took the bus or traveled outside of the neighborhood, you were 'properly covered up'.

Besides cleanliness being next to godliness, my mother was fierce about achieving your best in school. She often reminded me that average grades were for average kids and I was not an average kid! Coming home after school and turning on the TV was not something that was acceptable in our household. The rule was to come home from school and change your clothes (yes we changed clothes because what we wore to school was different from what we played in), get a snack, and do your homework. Once my mom got home from work, she checked our homework and any problems we had; she helped us. When it came to math, my mom deferred to my father, and while he didn't have the patience that mom had, he managed to help me pass algebra, trig., and physics.

The Queen had a system for us as her princesses. We knew that before we could go to bed, we had to clean up the kitchen and our bedrooms, lay out our clothes for school, and pack our backpacks. It did not please my mother to hear in the morning, "I need a glue stick or poster board for class today." Last minute was not welcomed in our house.

Once we were in bed, my mother would finish her chores, possibly work she brought home to complete, and whatever other tasks she deemed necessary before going to bed. I can count the times my mother was in bed before us.

Fast food restaurants were starting to pop up in our communities, but we were not acquainted with them because we ate home-cooked meals together on a daily basis. I know everyone is busy nowadays and it's easier to pick up something quick. But be aware that fast food meals are loaded with sodium, not to mention expensive. Depending on the age of your children (girls or boys), delegate dinner and kitchen chores! Cook a number of meals on the weekend, and when necessary, have your child heat up food for dinner during the week. Rotate the task, so that not only are daughters responsible for heating up dinner but also sons.

Sacrifice is not a word often used today by anybody, but putting your daughter's needs ahead of your own is something mothers should be accustomed to doing. For example, I knew women who had weekly hair appointments, yet their daughter's hair looked crazy. No! No! No! My mom went to the hairdresser when she could afford it, but every week she religiously shampooed and braided my sister's and my hair. On special occasions, we went to her hairdresser or my grandmother would wash and curl our hair. It was a ritual that I didn't look forward to, but it was something that was done on our behalf.

I don't remember my mother regularly buying clothes for herself. She always made sure we had what we needed first. In her mind, our needs were more important than hers.

And that included her time: Make yourself available to your daughter, so that when she needs or wants to talk about something or someone, she can come to you. We all know that women today are busy people. When my daughter was first born, I sold real estate. Once I realized that the majority of selling time was weekends and evenings, I quit selling real estate. If I didn't, I wouldn't see my daughter grow up. She was my sweetheart (my princess), and how could she grow up without her mom guiding her? Once she was older, I worked in corporate America. I traveled for the company, was an active church member and a member of a social organization that met a couple of times a month. However, I attended parent–teacher conferences, all of her concerts, and joined the parent booster band club to help raise money. I wasn't a perfect mom by any means, but I spent time with my daughter and shared my thoughts and dreams with her, as well as listening to her thoughts and dreams.

Her father and I divorced when she started high school, and you can imagine the 'fun' then in grooming an already hormonal female teen into a queen, and trying to influence someone who hates your guts because in her opinion you have broken up the family and have relocated her to another school away from her friends.

I kept my ego in check, brokered family conferences often between the three of us (she, her brother, and I), consistently parented instead of trying to be her friend, and loved her into adulthood. There was no subject that was off-limits, including why I divorced her father.

I encouraged her to invite her friends to our house, and hosted a number of teen parties. This gave me an opportunity to check out her peers, and on a few occasions I found myself saying "You might want to stay away from that girl, she's trouble."

As a divorced mom, I dated, but usually on the weekends my children spent with their father. My children (princess and prince) were my first priority. As a person of faith, I knew that children were a blessing and that I had a period of time to share my life, rules, and morals with them before they became adults.

When I think back on my years as a teen, my mom and dad ruled with an iron fist. I wasn't allowed to go out on Saturday night if I went out on Friday night. I had one friend with whom I could spend the night. My parents felt that I had a perfectly good bed at home; there was no need to spend the night at other girls' houses. Mom also felt that she had no idea what kind of moral character the other parents had so rather than put me in a compromising situation, I didn't spend the night out often.

If I was allowed to attend a party, I was driven there and picked up by one of my parents. If they were busy, I didn't go. As a high school student, my bedtime was 8:30pm. I was told I needed my rest, so that I would be productive in school. Years later when I asked my mom why I had to be in bed so early, she said she needed the time to regroup AND I needed the rest! Suffice to say, I never fell asleep in class!

Did I tell you about their dating rules? Well, they were pretty simple! I didn't date until I was sixteen. Mind you, I started high school early, so by the time I was sixteen, I was a junior. I was allowed to group date as a fifteen-year-old, as long as my parents knew the parents of all of the teens who were included in the group date. And, of course, I was driven to the event by my dad. The king, my dad, made it clear that I was not to ride in a "boy's car" without prior permission. Well, my father's exact words were: "I better not catch you in some boy's car!" Yikes!

Study Guide Questions for Oh, the Sacrifice:

1. Do you feel you currently make sacrifices for your daughter? If yes, explain how and why you make them.

2. What do you expect your daughter to do as a result of your sacrifices for her?

3. When you were 'growing up', did your mother make sacrifices for you? If yes, explain how you knew.

CHAPTER THREE

I WANT TO BE JUST LIKE *YOU*!

How many times did you say to yourself, "I want to be like my mom?" Often, right? I wanted to be a grownup—my mom's life seemed pretty glamorous to me, particularly when she was dressing to go out with my dad.

What I liked most was how she said what she was going to do and then did it. She was confident, she did what she wanted to do; and I admired that. As her princess, I wanted to be like HER! I was a dreamer, impulsive, pretty outspoken, and a gifted pianist. That was my raw talent. She took my talents and continuously placed me in situations that allowed me to use my skills and talents until I became the woman that I am today. As a young girl, I didn't think I was attractive like her, but she taught me that beauty was relative and temporary. She believed in brain power. A smart woman was a beautiful woman. It was important that I could think critically, make decisions for myself, read, write, and balance my checkbook. She also taught me the power of networking with other people to share what I have with other people as well.

Interestingly, my mother smoked cigarettes. My dad did too, for that matter. While I didn't think much of smoking (it made your hair and clothes smell), my first trip home from college, I pulled out a pack of cigarettes and lit one in front of my mother. She was horrified and asked me why I was smoking. I told her that she smoked, so it must be good enough for me. I tell that story because mothers, guess what? Your princesses watch everything you do: it doesn't matter what you say, it matters what you do. My mother showed me another side of her I was not aware of. She told me that she had smoked since she was nineteen years old, and if she could stop, she would. It was a terrible habit.

What a great lesson I learned from her. Don't do anything that you would not want your daughters to do (in front of you or behind your back). Be a person of integrity and honor. Be honest and admit your faults. There are enough societal pressures and influences for girls to be child beauty queens, video vixens, teen mothers, abused women, reality show women, and on and on.

Inspire your daughter to be like you. Be her shero. When she grows up, let her talk glowingly about her mother—you!

In some cultures, boys are revered and it is unpopular to have a daughter. That's unfortunate. If that is your experience, please instill all of your positive values into her. She cannot grow up properly without your guidance and wisdom. Create teachable moments where she learns the beauty of being a young woman. Teachable moments don't cost money, they just take time. Spend time with your precious gift called, daughter. I remember seeing the movie, 'Precious'. In the movie, Precious was a young woman who was mentally challenged, lived with her abusive mother, had been raped by her father, and bore two of his children. Her life appeared to be a terrible one, destined to fail. Her saving grace was a woman who believed in her and helped her become confident and educated, and to move away from her abusive mother. It was a great story; but what I couldn't understand was why her mother treated her so badly.

Sometimes we have our daughters at difficult times in our lives, and we tend to transfer the pain and stress onto our daughters. As females, we sometimes take on the weight of things that we shouldn't, feeling things like *My mother never wanted me, she prefers my brother*. Don't leave your daughter with that impression. I'm not saying that you have to pretend to be happy if you aren't; but carve out time for talking, sharing things that you like with her. Giving gifts like jewelry, cell phones, game systems, computers, clothing, and cars is not the same thing as giving your daughter your time and attention. A princess cannot turn into a queen without your help.

STUDY GUIDE QUESTIONS FOR

I WANT TO BE JUST LIKE *YOU*!

1. How have you responded to your daughter's requests to tag along with you? If yes, how; if no, why not:

2. What kinds of special time do you have with your daughter?

3. What kind of mother-daughter time did you share with your mother? How did you feel during these times?

CHAPTER FOUR

PROTECT HER INNOCENCE

What lengths would you go to protect a priceless gift? When it came to protecting my daughter, I did everything I could. I went to great lengths, because I didn't want her to tell me that someone (especially someone I trusted) molested her or acted inappropriately during her childhood.

In addition to screening her friends and their parents, I also screened TV shows and movies, music and videos. I listened to the latest songs (that she and her friends were listening to), and if I heard inappropriate language, it went onto the 'cannot listen to this list'. I would explain, but I also forbade most music videos because I never knew if the decent music videos were followed by the indecent ones. I didn't want to have my princess grow up faster than was necessary. I tried not to put her in situations where a male family member or friend would be alone with her. I know it sounds crazy, but in this day and age I would rather sound crazy than wish I had taken better precautions.

Also, I was selective with my princess in the rights of passage I allowed her to become involved in. She could wear clear fingernail polish at the age of seven, not earlier. Her clothes and shoes were age-appropriate. She played outside with the children in the neighborhood and was active in sports and dance. As a young girl, she was competitive and answered questions easily in class. As she approached middle school, I noticed that she was hesitant to answer questions, and so we discussed this. I knew that she knew the answers to the questions; what I didn't know was why she hesitated to answer the questions if boys were around.

Like my mother, I believed in girl brain power, and dumbing down was not encouraged in our household. Unfortunately, our society is more concerned with how women look than how they think and what they think. I remember my middle school years of loving science and not being very popular. But I don't regret for a minute learning about the physical world. It's also good to expose your princess to a number of different activities. One, because you never know if what you expose her to becomes her life's work; and two, "…An idle mind is the devil's workshop!" A phrase my grandmother used to illustrate how easy it was to get into trouble if you didn't have enough to do.

But what if I don't have the money to put my child into different activities? Well, investigate extracurricular activities in your daughter's school, check out the Boys and Girls club or Girl Scouts, contact a sorority in your area, and if you belong to a church, find out what the Youth group is doing. Fun does not have to cost money. You may find that you'll be asked to volunteer some time in exchange for your daughter's chance to join an organization.

Oh, the sacrifice! But that's just fine, right? (See Chapter Two!)

Shortly after I married, I was unsure whether I wanted to have children. So I contacted the Girl Scouts of America and was encouraged to help a local troop in my community. As you might just be able to guess, I ended up becoming the scout leader and had a wonderful three creative years of projects, cookie sales, and outdoor camping. I am not suggesting that you become a troop leader, but be open to opportunities to spend quality time with your daughter.

In addition to sharing the best that life had to offer with my daughter, I also used tragic moments as teachable moments. She was a tween when several young girls my daughter's age were run over by a truck. They were attending a sleepover and had decided to leave the house in the middle of the night. It was a horrible tragedy and I felt so bad for the parents of those girls. However, it was a teachable moment for my daughter as a mistake that could not be relived. I told her some mistakes you don't recover from. Right there was one of them.

How do you protect the innocence of your daughter as she becomes a teen? Don't try to be her friend: Give her house rules and abide by them. But don't talk at her: talk *with* her—and often. Listen, a lot! Give unconditional love. Attend her events. Say yes because you want to, not because you want her to like you.

Make sure she earns the privilege of what you are giving. It's amazing when parents tell me that their daughter acts like a spoiled brat, and yet they do nothing to insure that their daughter has earned what she gets. Just because a new cell phone or pair of shoes are out does not mean you have to buy them for your daughter. What has she done to earn them? Does she help out and contribute to the household? Is the kitchen cleaned up? Are the clothes washed/folded? Is her room cleaned? Has she completed her homework? Is dinner started? If not, why not? Giving your daughter chores around the house builds responsibility and teaches a simple equation for life: fulfilling your responsibilities = respect + reward.

Let me take a moment here and go back to listening. How often has your daughter told you something that you did not believe, only to find out that actually it was the truth? I remember when my daughter was in third or fourth grade and she told me that a man was following her (in his car) and her girlfriend to school. I didn't doubt her for a minute. We contacted the area police, as well as the school principal and Officer Friendly, the police officer assigned to her school. It was pretty scary, but the police apprehended the driver and his auto. We never got a straight answer on why he was following the girls, but it never occurred again. I sometimes wonder what would have happened if I hadn't listened to her and believed her.

Protecting my daughter's innocence also meant I was watchful of her feelings when people told her things I thought were psychologically harmful. I love family members! But what I don't understand is when they say insensitive things like "You're about as smart as your brother." or "Why would you go into a dumb field like psychology?" or "_____" … simply fill in the blank with any other completely stupid comment a family member has said over the years! While you may not be able to control Aunt Martha or Uncle Jack's comments, it's good to talk to your daughter to ensure that she doesn't absorb those harmful comments into her psyche.

That also goes for magazine, radio, and TV programs that promote beauty at all costs. Don't get me wrong, I love beautiful things and people. But I have a different perspective of beauty because of my upbringing. The skinniest, tallest model doesn't exemplify beauty to me. Is she healthy? Educated? A good manager of money? Thinks her own thoughts? Environmentally conscious? ... That's beauty in my eyes. Through discussions, reading magazines together, and volunteering time with agencies that help underprivileged people, I helped my daughter develop her own 'eyes' and determine what was beautiful.

I almost forgot to mention abusive boyfriends. Helping your daughter maintain her innocence also means that you monitor her behavior around her boyfriend. If she is unusually submissive, watch a little more closely to make sure he's not a bully. Of course, having a conversation about it is more open and holistic, but if you feel that she is giving you the typical teenage line of baloney, watch and listen for telltale signs of abuse.

I realize in some cultures, male domination is tolerated and often encouraged. In my opinion, domination is not synonymous with abuse. A male hitting a female is intolerable, no matter what the culture. So mothers, stop it from happening, stop it from developing— even at the first signs.

I just signed a petition to stop a New York advertiser from taking prostitution ads. Many teen girls are being human trafficked. Human trafficking is the illegal trade of human beings for the purposes of commercial or sexual exploitation or forced labor—a modern-day form of slavery. When I was a girl, prostitutes were grown women who chose prostitution to put food on the table for their families, or who found it as a quick way to make money, or who were forced into it because they were kidnapped as young girls.

It is your responsibility to grow your princess into a queen. That means she has to grow up in a safe environment. If you cannot guarantee that in your household, consider moving her someplace that can ensure her safety.

STUDY GUIDE QUESTIONS FOR

PROTECT HER INNOCENCE:

---

1. Were you protected in your childhood? Explain how. If not, give an example of when you felt unprotected.

2. Was there ever a time that a male family member or family friend touched you inappropriately? If yes, please explain.

3. If you answered yes to Question 2, did you tell your mother? If no, please explain how you handled it.

CHAPTER FIVE

SHE'S AS CLOSE AS SKIN

How often have you looked up and noticed your daughter standing as close to you as possible? It happened often with me, and unless I was really out of sorts, I thoroughly enjoyed the time we spent together. Before her brother was born, we were constant companions. As a matter of fact, I knew every word to the Little Mermaid movie. I think I've seen that movie at least fifty times!

This is an opportune time to build great customs and treasured moments that they will remember for a lifetime. For Halloween, we both used to dress up and give out candy at the door. If your daughter loves dolls, make doll clothes with her and play dress up the dolls. Plan a tea party! Play hopscotch together, or go to the local pond and watch the ducks. Depending on your age, you may be unfamiliar with these 'ancient' games! But make up games and fun times that you both will enjoy. Have *fun* together! What I don't want you to do is to resort to and 'hide' behind today's electronic games where no *communication* takes place between you and your daughter.

If your idea of hanging out involves eating out (one of my favorite things to do!), be sure to choose healthy places, so that you both don't pick up weight while having fun. If you or your daughter is overweight, make it a project to lose weight together. Depending on the age of your daughter, dieting is frowned upon unless she is quite overweight. However, working out together with a workout video, walking or running together and eating healthy foods that are nutritious and low-calorie is another way to spend time with each other.

My daughter was very in tune with my moods and spirit. If I was worried about something, she seemed even closer than usual. Maybe it was the amount of time we spent together (or possibly we traveled together in other lifetimes; I sometimes wonder about that. Who knows?) Even now, it is not surprising when I receive a call from my princess, asking "Are you okay, I had a dream about you..." More often than not, something was happening in my life that I had not shared with her, and being close as skin, meant she picked up my *vibration* as it were.

This quality time spent together while she was young was also my admission to her private life as she became an adolescent and teen. You see, your children want YOU when they are young. They want as much of you as you can give them. Once they reach the stage where the opinions of their peers matter more to them than your opinion of them, the door to their inner life has closed. If you have been an important inhabitant, then you will still be welcomed, just not as often.

Did I mention that you also have to be trustworthy? What I mean here firstly is that you do what you say you will do: you uphold the rules and you consistently parent. But you also know how to have fun and if you are told a secret, you know how to keep that secret.

Being close as skin does not mean that you get to invade your daughter's privacy. I know mothers who go through their daughter's email, cell phone, diary, letters, etc. I didn't do that. If I felt something was amiss with my daughter, I asked her about it. I watched how she acted around the house and her friends, so I usually knew when something wasn't quite right. Now, I realize there are mother/daughter relationships where honesty and trustworthiness is not the norm. Don't get me wrong, if after talking with my princess, I still needed to go through her things, I would have. I wouldn't have felt good about it, sure; but I would be doing it out of love and concern.

If you have honesty and trust issues in your relationship, I recommend that you consider help from a therapist. It can really help in starting to slowly rebuild your relationship with your daughter.

Make sure you spend a few minutes daily, doing something together—even if it's something fairly routine like getting dinner together for the family.

Quality time is a love language, where a person shows how much they love you by giving you their time. Maybe one of your daughter's love languages is quality time. It is certainly one of mine. Perhaps words of encouragement or small gifts are ways you show that you care. After all these years, I believe my mother's love language was acts of service.[1] Taking good care of us was important to her. It didn't always address my need to spend time or hear words of encouragement. So make sure your princess knows she's loved. Put a scented note on her pillow sometimes, so that as she is getting into bed, she will see it. Maybe that sounds a little different? But think how you would feel if you were the one getting the message of love. Right? And in our modern world, how about this: Send love text messages to your daughter. You know how to send text messages, right? If not, ask her! Or a friend can easily show you. Actually, most youths today can show you how to send text messages. Youth & technology! Amazing! By the way, cell phones don't stay in your daughter's room overnight, especially while they are in middle school or high school. Notice that I didn't say grammar school. Grammar school-aged girls don't need cell phones at all—just my opinion! Princesses need a good night's sleep, and by keeping their phones you ensure they get that.

---

[1] Dr. Gary Chapman, author of The 5 Love Languages®

STUDY GUIDE QUESTIONS FOR

SHE'S AS *CLOSE AS SKIN*:

1. Write down several experiences where you have noticed the closeness of your daughter. Be specific.

2. Were you close to your mother? How did she handle your closeness?

3. Practice having two close times each week. Write down what you did and how you felt afterward.

CHAPTER SIX

TELL HER THE TRUTH

As women, we have so many secrets, don't we? I know I do. As a rule, secrets are not bad. However, some experiences that we have had as women should be shared with younger women (our girls) to be used as teachable moments, and to hopefully prevent mistakes from being repeated.

Obvious experiences could be divorce, having a child out of wedlock, having an extramarital affair, having an abortion, running away from responsibility, shoplifting, or using/abusing drugs. These events are not ones we are proud to own up to, and yet if we lived through them, they are a testimony to God's amazing grace in our life. We did not have our life experiences to keep them a secret and take them to our grave. Maybe telling your life story to your daughter (or other young women in your life) may help her avoid making the same mistakes.

Well, what if my daughter loses respect for me? What if she never speaks to me again? What do I do? That's a big risk and while it could happen, most likely it will not happen. Children have forgiven parents for greater mistakes than the ones listed at the beginning of this chapter. It may take a number of conversations before she can talk about your experiences in a way that pleases you, but remember why you told her. This kind of sharing of intimate information about your life is not something you plan to share just for grins. Clearly your daughter is heading in the wrong direction, and your hope is to point her in the proper direction. For example, your adolescent daughter has been withdrawn lately, and is coming home from school an hour or two late several times a week. You try talking with her, and she tells you nothing is wrong. Well, clearly something is wrong or she would be coming home from school at a normal time. It might be a good idea to show up unannounced at her school to give her a ride home.

Let's say that she's not at school, and you find out that she's ditched school. Now you have a problem. Do you know who her close friends are? Think back to your adolescent years. Did you skip school to hang out with friends before going home?

Think about how you want to handle this scenario before you see your daughter. You may want to strangle her, but of course that's not the answer, not to mention it's rather against the law! Seriously though, this is a great opportunity to try out your parenting skills in dealing with a stressful situation without losing your cool. Once you find your daughter and start talking, be sure to share your own adolescent experiences with her. Be sure to tell her how you felt when you didn't know where she was. Talk about how crazy our society is and how she could have been kidnapped and sold on the underground market as a child slave. Use this experience as a teachable moment. Once you two have discussed this thoroughly, be sure to tell her what the consequences are for failing to come home at the time you expected her, and execute those consequences—she is grounded.

Telling your daughter the truth also means that you answer her questions honestly. Lying to her will only backfire, probably when you least expect it. I knew a woman who adopted her daughter when she was six months old. She adored her and was a good mother to her. She had always said that when her daughter was older, she would tell her that she was adopted. Only, there never seemed to be the right time to tell her about the adoption. Well, the girl was in a car accident and as a result of the injuries that she sustained, she needed a blood transfusion. Neither one of her parents' blood type matched the daughter's. Of course, the time had come to tell their daughter that she was adopted.

She was devastated, and asked what other things had they kept from her. It was a messy situation and took several months before the daughter was able to forgive them for keeping an important fact like adoption from her.

How do you feel about honestly telling your daughter what you think of her or something she's doing? I believe this is an area where we as mothers fall down continuously. We either err on the side of saying too much, or we say too little. There has to be a happy medium.

Here is an example: Your daughter is the head of her school's cheerleader squad, and on several occasions you have overheard her being very degrading when talking to or about members of the cheerleading team. Do you: 1) Talk to her and encourage her to treat her teammates as she would like to be treated? Or 2) Do you decide she's a chip off the old block and you secretly admire how she holds her ground with the other girls? Maybe you weren't as popular in school as your daughter, so you admire how she treats the other girls. But what's to admire about talking in degrading ways? Remember she is a princess in training, and what she does reflects on your training of her. Help her understand that a leader treats people fairly and honorably. Let her know that denigrating others is never acceptable behavior.

Do you have to share every private part of your life? Not at all. You are the judge of what information you will share with your daughter. But don't wait for a disaster as the reason you decide to share a part of your life with your princess. After all, you don't want her to repeat the mistakes you have made and you want her to grow up healthy, whole, and wise.

STUDY GUIDE QUESTIONS FOR

TELL HER THE TRUTH:

1. Do you have secrets that you have not shared with your daughter? What kind(s)? Why haven't you shared them?

2. Are they secrets that you would consider sharing if you thought they would be beneficial to your daughter's growth as a young woman? How do you think talking about them might help her?

3. Did you feel that your mother had secrets that would have been beneficial for you to know? Please explain.

CHAPTER SEVEN

NURTURING HER VS. RAISING HER

What do you think of when you hear the word 'nurture'? To me, nurture means to take care of something or someone in soothing ways. Nurture also means to cherish or encourage. Do you speak words of encouragement when you talk to your daughter? Do you tell her you love her, or do you expect her to know that you love her because you provide a roof over her head and clothes for her to wear? Maybe you weren't raised to express your emotions. Is it possible that your grandmother was the only person who told you she loved you? Maybe your dad told you too, but when your grandmother told you she loved you, she hugged you really tight and you felt like the single most wonderful person in the world.

When I was growing up, my mom did not tell me she loved me. She took care of my siblings and I in many ways, but telling us she loved us just wasn't something she did. She later told me her mom wasn't demonstrative either, so the words *I love you* were not often said, if said at all.

In some cultures, the children (males and females) are hugged, kissed, and told how loved they are many times. I believe that this familial type of love and nurturing allows you to grow up confidently. You don't feel that you have to find love in all the wrong places, like in an abusive relationship. When you have been nurtured throughout your life, you may decide not to have children until you can afford to love, cherish and nurture them within the confines of a committed relationship.

What is the opposite of nurturing your daughter? Sure, literally the opposite of nurturing your daughter would be to starve or neglect her. But I also believe the opposite of nurturing your daughter is to raise her without the tenderness and temperance that you might give to your favorite friend or relative. Raising your daughter means you tell her what to do, you admonish (correct) her when she does something wrong, and you make sure that she is self-sufficient. Technically, she can maneuver throughout life in an efficient way. However, she is emotionally bare. She needs your acceptance, words of encouragement, hugs, love, and lots of I

LOVE YOUs! Remember how good you felt when that favorite person in your family told you they loved you? You felt special and always wanted to be around them. Do the same thing for your princess. What better way to prepare her to raise her royal subjects than to give her your love, *show* her your love, and *tell* her often how much you love her. Don't be the type of mother who is able to love and *nurture* her son, but only *raises* her daughter.

How do you start? Well, give her a hug and say the words – "I really love you." If you aren't used to saying *I love you*, it may sound foreign and fake. Don't worry; practice saying it often until the words *I love you* become comfortable to you. What if your teen daughter tells you to leave her alone? You know, "Ew Mom, what are you doing?" Don't worry about it, that's just teenage language for, "I don't understand this gesture and I'm embarrassed."

In my first book, "Trying to Stay Sane While Raising Your Teen", I talk about the importance of controlling our tempers and language when interacting with our teens. The same advice is true when dealing with our daughters at any age. I knew a woman who didn't believe in corporal punishment (spanking), but she didn't mind giving her daughters a real cursing out if she thought it would help them behave. I have also heard mothers yell and berate their daughters, and I felt bad hearing that tirade, so I can only imagine how the daughters felt.

Am I telling you not to yell, scream, curse, or spank? That's up to you. What I am saying is that if that is normally how you interact with your princess, then understand that is how she will respond to others (including her future children). Remember that our children model our behavior. If that is what you want, okay continue to yell, scream, or curse. Notice that I did not include spank in my last sentence. My mother (and father) included spanking in their arsenal of parenting tools. I didn't spank my daughter often, but occasionally her behavior warranted a spanking. Timeout may work exceptionally well, as does taking away privileges.

All I am encouraging you to do is to be mindful of how you dole out whatever corrective behavior mechanisms you plan to use.

It is extremely important to talk and listen to your daughter, especially when you are correcting her behavior. She needs to know that, at the end of the day, she is still the light of your life and nothing she does can take your love for her away. I believe that's how our Creator treats us: *Nurturing* vs. *raising*.

STUDY GUIDE QUESTIONS FOR

NURTURING HER VS. *RAISING* HER:

1. How important to you is having a good relationship with your daughter?

2. What does 'having a good relationship' with your daughter mane to you?

3. What do you say to her when you are disappointed in something she has done?

4. How do you treat her when you are delighted with something she has done?

5. What kind of relationship did you have with your mother?

CHAPTER EIGHT

THE SEXUALITY STORM

Do you think of your daughter as a young flower that slowly blossoms with the petals opening as she grows and matures? It's a nice analogy, isn't it? The problem is there can be a lot of storms on the way: your princess's sexuality perhaps the *tsunami* amongst them.

Traditionally, 'nice girls' weren't sexual. They wore appropriate clothing: skirts weren't too short or tight and the shorts weren't too short. And 'good girls' didn't wear make-up until they were upperclassmen in high school (unless they had a job), and they certainly carried themselves respectfully around boys. There were very few pregnant teens, and if they found themselves 'in the family way', they might have been shipped off to Aunt Doris' house down south to have the baby without embarrassing the family.

While I am not naïve enough to believe that the majority of the teen pregnancies are caused by girls who were not loved or hugged enough, I believe some of these pregnancies could be avoided if parents, particularly mothers, pay attention to the signals that their teenage daughters give when they are about to do something stupid, like having early-age sex! I admit the allure of having forbidden sex is a strong one. In some cases, all of the talking in the world doesn't stop the raging female hormones from colliding with the raging male hormones. But I bet a conversation about sexually transmitted diseases and life-long parenting commitments may be enough to cool those out of control hormones.

My mother had a short conversation with my sister and I— *Don't bring home any babies!* While that was a short conversation, she talked with each of us (separately) about how our bodies were changing from that of a girl's body to that of a young woman's. She had the birds & bees conversation with us and allowed me to ask anything having to do with my body and my urges. She also suggested that I visit the local clinic to get birth control pills if I felt I wanted to have 'forbidden' sex.

While this may sound permissive to you, whatever your beliefs hundreds of young girls are having unwanted pregnancies, and most of these girls may have been able to prevent them with a few more direct conversations and a more watchful eye from their mothers. Princesses lose their way, just like you and me. Remember, you are training your young princess to become a well-informed queen. She cannot be well-informed without your words of wisdom, honest guidance, and listening ear.

It's also important to point out the enhanced sexuality that society imposes on women and our girls in particular, that forces our daughters to appear to be more mature than they really are. A good example is when I used to shop for my eldest daughter. When she was a young girl, I found wonderful dresses and outfits that allowed her look like *la jeune fille* (the young girl) that she was. I was able to find age-appropriate clothing until she reached eleven years old. But after age eleven, the clothes were no longer clean-cut, wholesome outfits that adolescent girls wore. They looked a lot more provocative. I could not understand why a twelve-year-old had to have low-cut dresses with splits, or pants that were too tight. We actually thought about commissioning a clothing designer to make clothes for adolescent and pre-teen girls. By the time we had an idea of who would create the clothing, though, our daughter was no longer in that in-between stage of dressing.

On another note related to sexuality: Did I mention that music videos were outlawed in my home? My thought was that I did not want my daughter (or son) and their friends watching teens and young adults gyrating across the TV screen singing songs about sex. I heard a pastor say that age fifteen–twenty-four was a time of preparation for young people, not a time for having babies! Monitor what kinds of influences you allow to come in contact with your daughter.

When I started high school, we were not allowed to wear pants, though they were slowly being introduced into the dress code. My mother was very much against me wearing pants (particularly jeans) to school because she was afraid that if I wore casual clothes to school, my demeanor would be casual. I had to promise that I would sit like a lady and not like a guy (with my legs open). What a mother I had! I also didn't wear make-up until I took senior yearbook pictures. Her biggest concern about what I wore was that she did not want me to attract the attention of men. I was a young girl going through puberty, and that was a headache enough for her (and me) without the unwanted advances of men. Ugh!

Nowadays, there seems to be less concern with our daughters having unwanted contact with men. I was pretty strict with my daughter's contact with male friends of the family, and with distant male relatives. Since it was hard to tell who was trustworthy and who wasn't, we had a limited number of male family members and friends whose car our daughter was allowed to ride in without us. Call me paranoid, but I didn't want my daughter to tell me that Randall, the family friend molested her because we trusted him around our daughter. If you are dating, be careful of the contact that your male friend has with your daughter. And mothers, if your daughter tells you that her dad or uncle is coming into her room at night—believe her! Protect her and her sexuality.

Another area of concern is teen dating and the violence that often takes place. Teen dating violence is **real**! Below are several facts about teen dating violence:

- Did you know that only 33% of teens who were in abusive relationships, told anyone about it?[2]
- About 40% of teenage girls aged 14–17 say they know someone their age who have been hit, beaten, kicked, or slapped by a boyfriend. [3]
- Six out of ten rapes of young women occur in their own home or a friend or relative's home, not in a dark alley.[4]
- A recent survey of schools found there were an estimated 4,000 incidents of rape or other types of sexual assault in public schools across the country.[5]
- Approximately 80% of girls who have been victims of physical abuse in their dating relationships continue to date the abuser.[6]
- Nearly 20% of teen girls who have been in a relationship said that their boyfriend had threatened violence or self-harm in the event of a break-up.[7]

I was pretty quiet about my friends, especially the boys I liked, because I had serious dating restrictions, and I felt that the

---

[2] http://www.dosomething.org/tipsandtools/11-facts-about-youth-dating-violence/6-7-2012
[3] ibid
[4] ibid
[5] ibid
[6] http://womensissues.about.com/od/datingandsex/a/TeenDatingAbuse.htm
[7] ibid

less my parents knew, the better. In our household, dating a member of the opposite sex began only at age sixteen. The problem that I had was that I was thirteen when I started high school, and most of my high school experience would be over by the time I reached sixteen.

What I was allowed to do, though, was 'group date'. Group dating was pretty 'harmless' because my parents knew everyone in the group, including my friends' parents. I was dropped off and picked up by my mother or father, so I seldom had an opportunity to be alone with a hormone-raging boy! To be honest, it was a great idea because while some of my friends had permissive parents, as a group we stayed together either at someone's home, skating, bowling or at the movies. And for a young-un (a phrase my grandmother called me) it allowed me to take my time getting to know how boys acted.

High school for me, compared to high school for my daughter today is light years apart in terms of the laxity that some parents exhibit and in societal norms. During my high school years, my mom was shrewd enough to know when I was doing something that I shouldn't. I wasn't allowed to ride in cars with young men unless it was a special date, like prom. I remember receiving a friendship bracelet as a gift from a boy for Valentine's Day. My mother saw it and made me give it back! While I am sure, teen dating violence existed back then, fact is none of my high school girlfriends experienced it.

One of my daughter's middle school friends was sleeping around with several of the basketball team members and as a well-intentioned mother, I called her mother and told her. She did not believe me and told me in no uncertain terms to mind my own business! It cost me our friendship because she didn't speak to me again; but what about her daughter? Didn't she want to have an authentic and honest relationship with her daughter? What was her daughter missing that caused her to want to have casual sex as a thirteen-year-old?

As a high school teacher, I spoke with students who were in relationships with other teens, experiencing intimate relationships and also experiencing violence. It was not a subject they were comfortable talking about at home.

Beth, another mother I spoke with, mentioned that she is also quite protective of her daughter and her daughter's sexuality. While her daughter is in high school, she can only group date until she demonstrates the maturity her parents feel she needs in order to date.

By the way, how much older than your daughter should her boyfriend be? Or rather, *not* be! Check out the teen dating quiz below. I found this quiz helpful in determining if your daughter is friends with a boy or is actually dating him.[8]

1. How many times does your teen talk to the friend in a given week?

☐ All the time.

☐ 2-4 times a week.

☐ Maybe once a week.

☐ None.

8
http://parentingteens.about.com/library/sp/quiz/dating/blteen_dating_quiz.htm

2. Does your teen try to hide their conversation with their friend?

☐ Yes.

☐ No.

☐ Sometimes.

☐ Not sure.

3. Have you caught your teen and their friend holding hands or kissing?

☐ Yes.

☐ No.

☐ Sometimes.

☐ Not sure.

4. Do they do things together, like go to the movies, with other friends?

☐ Yes.

☐ No.

☐ Sometimes.

☐ Not sure.

5. Has your teenager stopped seeing other friends in favor of spending time with this friend?

☐ Yes.

☐ No.

☐ Sometimes.

☐ Not sure.

How did you answer the questions? If your answers reveal that it looks like your princess is dating, then here are some things to consider to help avoid a *tsunami*: Have you met the young man your daughter is dating? Does he come to the door and ring the bell (like all good dates did on the Cosby Show!), or does he beep the horn for your daughter to come out for their date? What are you teaching her to expect from a young man? Have you explained how she is to handle herself so that she is not another dating violence statistic?

Our daughters experience these unhealthy relationship behaviors sometimes right underneath our noses without our knowledge. But without our wise guidance, how can they know how to proceed?

Mothers, WAKE UP! Your daughters need to be able to talk and be comfortable about talking with you on any subject—whether it's considered 'taboo' or not.

STUDY GUIDE QUESTIONS FOR

THE SEXUALITY STORM:

1. When you were a young girl, what were you allowed to do with and around your father?

2. Were you allowed to walk around in your underwear?

3. Did you sit on your dad's lap? How old were you before that was no longer acceptable?

4. What are your sexuality views when it comes to your daughter?

5. What ground rules have you established with your daughter for dating?

CHAPTER NINE

YOUR FATHER LOVES YOU
MORE THAN ME

While this topic did not occur in my family, I had close teenage girlfriends who constantly competed with their moms for their dad's attention. In some cases, my friends' mothers wore clothes and make-up similar to ours, and competed with us—making access to dad difficult. There was a lot of jealousy and it was hard to feel comfortable when I was around my friend and her mother.

There is something breathtaking about our little girls growing into young women, isn't there? We all believe that our daughters are beautiful; face it, some girls are absolutely drop-dead gorgeous! As the mother of a physically beautiful daughter, you have to remember that beauty is in the eye of the beholder. Most girls think they are ugly, too thin, too fat, too short or tall, or something (*any*thing!) is wrong with them. While everyone believes their daughter is beautiful, including you, there are also women who believe that their husbands are more attracted to their daughters (sick, right?) than to them. Hence, "Your dad loves you more than me."

In many families, the daughter gravitates to one parent or the other. Depending on the age of your daughter, she may start out as your little partner, and then spend more time with your husband as she grows up. All of these situations are acceptable as long as your daughter's needs are met. When I became a teen, I spent more time with my mother; but we started butting heads as I reached my sixteenth birthday, and I found it easier to talk to my dad. I suppose if your husband and daughter were spending unusual amounts of time together that should make you wonder why. My advice is to share yourself with your daughter, be available, and be open and easy to talk to. She may be a daddy's girl, but do watch those favorite movies of hers over and over, play dolls, paint nails, and create time with her to form those uniquely *you two* times. Men can't turn princesses into queens, the way moms can. It's not impossible especially since there are many single dads raising children. However at some point, a daughter needs a positive female role model to help shape her into the woman she will become.

It occurred to me that men see us in our daughters. They see the youth and fresh beauty that we once exhibited. I say 'once' exhibited. It doesn't have to be once, of course. You can continue to be beautiful and youthful. Raising children is challenging, but moms, remember to take time to refresh yourself. Treat yourself to a hot bubble bath or put on a little perfume, blush and lip gloss before you leave the house. We forget that our men are visual and there are lots of female distractions, so continue to take care of you: eat healthy foods, exercise, and take time for yourself. Then as our daughters grow into young, beautiful women, we won't feel insecure about our looks, because our inner beauty will still shine through!

STUDY GUIDE QUESTIONS FOR YOUR FATHER LOVES YOU MORE THAN ME:

1. When you were a young girl, which parent did you follow most of the time?

2. What kind of message did your mother communicate to you about your physical appearance?

3. How well did you get along with the kids in your neighborhood? In your school classes?

CHAPTER TEN

ANTAGONISM AND CONFLICT

What is it about the mother/daughter relationship, which makes it so hard to get along? While I respected and obeyed my mother most of the time, on occasions I would argue with her (or at least hold a grudge). However, if my dad told me what to do, I generally did it without any argument or ill feelings. And this feeling followed me into my twenties. Why is that?

Antagonism, as defined by Webster is "mutual enmity, hostility."[9]

I have also have overheard conversations from mothers to their daughters. The harsh and mean spirited words that were spoken were devastating and hurt my heart. All I could think was "Is that how you show love to your daughter, your princess?" And of course, your daughter is learning by the example that you have set for her, so of course she will be mean and harsh to her friends, and possibly dispassionate with her children. I overheard Angelic tell her daughter how stupid she was, and I'm paraphrasing her

---

[9] Webster's II New Riverside Dictionary, revised edition. 1996 by Houghton Mifflin.

words to protect my reading audience! I was horrified at how much like a knife her words must have felt to her daughter. When I think of mothers, I think of love, compassion, support, home, and unconditional acceptance. If my mom talks to me with contempt and disgust, (and she is my source of love and acceptance), where do I go for love, acceptance, and compassion?

If that kind of antagonism has been going on since your daughter was a young girl, then when she reaches her teen years, she is going to be full of anger and antagonism.

Before I paint a picture of animosity and antagonism being learned from mothers, I also know that even in the best mother/daughter relationships, as the daughter reaches puberty, or as the old folks used to say, "You're smelling yourself," your daughter begins to treat you like you are day-old milk. You no longer know anything of value, and she doesn't want to be around you.

I think what was really going on was that I would always approach my experiences and challenges differently than my mother would. I was a free-spirit. She was organized and highly disciplined. I took risks, and her preferred way of handling things was to write pros & cons. Neither way was the wrong way! Yet I grew up respecting my mother, but disliking her at the same time.

I saw my mother not as a human (with feelings), but as a machine that could do anything as long as she had a plan. She was emotionless (most times), functional, but there were no chinks in her armor, and she appeared to be infallible. But I could never seem to please her. So I usually kept a respectable distance from Mom. She wasn't a mean person, quite the opposite. She meant business, 24/7, but she never heaped on statements like, "You're stupid," "You're nothing like your sister," "You're such a f*@#up!" There are women who say hateful words like these to their daughters (sons too) and those words may as well be knives, because they cut out your life source and damage your self-esteem.

"A working mother-daughter relationship is a powerful tool in the shaping of future generations and present families."[10] Allow me to be more dramatic and say that women are the core of families; we are the nurturers and as such, pass on the traits of love, authenticity, faith, compassion, trust, human kindness, and orderliness to our daughters and sons. This in no way discounts a man's ability to be a nurturer, but it does mean that women, as the bearers of children, carry the primary responsibility for teaching these traits to our children. How many times have you heard that wars would not be fought if women ran the world? You don't grow up yelling and cursing to your children, if you didn't learn it firsthand. What better way to teach our girls love and compassion than to treat them with love and compassion?

Women used to talk about how uncomfortable they were while they were pregnant. I decided that that would not be my reality, so while I was pregnant I would talk to my unborn baby:

---

[10] Raising Homemakers, http://raisinghomemakers.com/2011/mothers-and-daughters/6/7/2012

one, to get to know it; and two, to reassure my baby that I would love him/her with my entire being. Once she was born, we spent time together, and I used words of love when I talked to her. I enjoyed her and she knew it. It doesn't mean that we didn't have times of conflict. Of course we did. However, our relationship was built on love *first*. Not only did I tell her daily that I loved her, I showed her I loved her by spending time with her, playing with her, and talking to and with her. Our relationship was secure and she knew that if I had to discipline her, it was merely a consequence of something she did; it wasn't because I was having a bad day and she just got in the way of my feelings.

Often antagonism builds up between mothers and daughters when mothers continuously criticize their daughters. For example, Gwen is in her late twenties; she dreads when her mother comes to visit because her mother always finds something wrong with Gwen or her home. Neither woman is comfortable enough to honestly say what they are feeling, so the feelings are never expressed; but the animosity and resentment stay in the air whenever Gwen and her mother are around each other.

The relationship between a mother and her daughter is a beautiful one—or at least it *should* be. If you and your mother can barely tolerate each other, begin by forgiving her silently for what you perceive were issues she caused, and issues you caused. (Remember there are always two sides to any 'story'.) Next, arrange time when you can talk to each other without any interruptions (*turn off your cell phone*). Once you two are together, agree to hear each other out, be respectful, and have an honest conversation. You may be able to have one conversation that clears the air and allows you to begin interacting with your mother in ways you previously were unable to do. It may take several conversations, depending on the amount of resentment and walls that exist between the two of you, but give yourselves time to talk, love, and heal.

If your mother is deceased or you are unable to make contact with her, take time to meditate on your relationship with your mother, or write your experiences in a journal (daily), until you are able to release the antagonism, anger, and resentment that you experienced with her. This process will take time, especially depending on how much emotional turmoil you experienced.

Don't be surprised if some of your unhealthy habits surface during these purging sessions. You may want to eat 'comfort' foods, things like chocolate, French fries, candy, etc. or you may find that a neat martini or glass of Scotch helps you through this process. Be careful not to resolve one problem (mentally repairing your relationship with your mother) and pick up another one— weight gain or overdependence on alcohol or other substances. Reward yourself in other ways by getting a pedicure or a scented bubble bath, or maybe treating yourself to a new (affordable!) purchase at your favorite store. We're women, right…? We can shop!

STUDY GUIDE QUESTIONS FOR

ANTAGONISM AND CONFLICT:

1. What kind of relationship did you have with your mother and grandmother?

2. Do you enjoy the relationship that you have with your mother? How? Why?

3. If the relationship with your mother was not a positive one and your mother is deceased or unknown, list the steps you will take to repair your feelings.

CHAPTER ELEVEN

OUTSPOKEN...? OH YES!

"Mom, you don't know what you're talking about."

Did your daughter just talk back to you? Or is she just outspoken? The Merriam Webster dictionary defines 'outspoken' as "direct and open in speech or expression,"[11] while 'back talk' is "impudent, insolent, or argumentative replies."[12] We want our daughters to speak confidently with their peers and colleagues, but how do they learn this important skill if they can't speak their minds with us?

I remember the first time my oldest daughter spoke her young mind (I think she was four years old), my mother said I was too permissive and would later regret letting my daughter get away with talking so "disrespectfully" to me. I worried a bit, as young mothers do, when their mothers express displeasure in something they have done. However, I thought back to my years as a child. My parents were strict disciplinarians, so as kids we were careful how we expressed our opinions. Even with that, usually at dinner,

---

[11] http://www.merriam-webster.com/dictionary/outspoken 7/3/2012
[12] http://www.merriam-webster.com/dictionary/backtalk

we would talk freely about anything that was going on in our lives. My parents recognized that the less we talked, the less they knew what we were thinking and what was going on in our world. They encouraged us to speak out. The one overriding rule was that we had to be respectful—no profanity. While I opened up a bit, there were still things I didn't share with my mother (or father).

Today, I know some mothers who are more concerned with appearances, so if an outspoken daughter makes them look bad, they don't want to allow 'real talk' to occur. They perceive their friends will feel that they don't have control of their children, and that look really bad!

I encourage those mothers and everyone else to find a safe place for both daughters and mothers to communicate comfortably about anything and everything. It doesn't help your daughter if she is allowed to tell you about her school day, but she can't talk about her sexuality, her desire to get high or her blow-up at her teacher. It also doesn't help her if you don't allow her to speak out as a young girl, because if she can't speak out, then she cannot develop her voice for her teen and adult years.

All of that aside, I will tell you what I did *not* allow... If you have an opinion, feel free to state it. Please do not talk under your breath!

You know what I'm talking about, right? You tell your daughter to change outfits because no respectable daughter of yours is going out dressed like she is! She says, "I can go out dressed any way I want." Only, she didn't say it out loud; no she whispered it under her breath. Nope—unacceptable behavior!

STUDY GUIDE QUESTIONS FOR

OUTSPOKEN...? OH YES!:

1. How did you communicate with your mother?

2. Was it safe to speak honestly and openly to your mother, grandmother, or aunts?

3. What ways does your daughter communicate with you?

CHAPTER TWELVE

ADVISE NOW OR CRY LATER

It's amazing the sacrifices we have to make as mothers. Once you become a mother, your life is never your own again. Even when your children grow up and move away, your life is forever changed. That's not a bad thing though.

I also believe that wisdom is earned. Ideally by the time you become a mom, you have had experiences you can share with your daughters. We don't have these experiences, good or bad, to hide them away and keep them secret. God expects us to share those experiences in the hopes that some mistakes can be avoided by our daughters.

Have you ever wondered what 'generational sins' meant? According to Spiritual Warfare Ministries, "Generational curses are judgments that are passed on to individuals because of sins perpetuated in a family in a number of generations. Generational curses are similar to original sin curses because they can be passed down on a generational basis."[13]

---

[13] http://www.sw-mins.org/gen_curses.html – 7/11/12

I think the sins of the mother can be passed down to the daughter(s) and the daughter's daughters when women refuse to own up to their own mistakes and share that wisdom with their daughters. This of course assumes that you are a faith-based person. If you are not, then generational sins make no sense whatsoever. However, how do you explain generations of infidelity, drug abuse, or bearing children out of wedlock? It doesn't just occur. The scenes are committed to memory and repeated over and over and over. Remember it is not what you *say* to your daughter that she mimics; it's what she *sees* you do that she will most often imitate.

That's one extreme. The other extreme is when you decide that you want to protect your daughter from all of the sordid secrets that exist within the family, so you don't to tell her about the family skeletons, like Aunt Mable sleeping with her son-in-law and having a child by him. The skeletons may not affect your life personally but family skeletons still need to be known and shared with your offspring. You are sharing this information for two reasons: First, it is family history, and second, if she has an experience that she wants to keep secret, she will feel more comfortable sharing it with you and/or her daughters. I had a woman tell me that a chest was found in the basement of their family home; inside of the chest were the remains of a baby. First of all, who would leave a baby in a chest, and secondly what kind of parenting required that if you got pregnant, you could not share that information with anyone, so you had to hide it away?

Yes, it is our job to protect our daughters, but sometimes protection means sharing experiences that we are ashamed of. I was often at odds with my first husband because I was brutally honest when it came to discussions with our children about our lives and the lives of our relatives. My family had skeletons, but I knew about them; they weren't kept secret until a relative was on his or her deathbed.

Finding out that your cousin is really your half-sister is not helpful the summer you are headed to college, and it was a well-kept family secret prior to that time. Taking a blood test and finding out you are adopted when you are getting married is not cool either. If you were molested as a child, I suggest that you find a therapist to talk to. Additionally, consider sharing that information with your daughter once you think she's old enough to understand what you are saying, and the impact that that trauma had on your life.

Trust takes time to develop between mothers and daughters. When our daughters are infants, they rely on us for everything, so trust is built-in. As her needs become more complex, trust continues to grow based on your availability to your daughter and how you respond to her during tough times.

I am not advising you to tell all! What I do advise is sharing your experiences privately with your daughter when you think it necessary and appropriate, and explaining that while we as mothers makes mistakes, you hope she doesn't have to make the same mistakes you made.

STUDY GUIDE QUESTIONS FOR

ADVISE NOW OR CRY LATER:

1. Were there family secrets in your family?

2. What age were you when the secrets were shared with you? Who shared the secrets? Why?

3. Are you holding any secrets that you have not shared with your daughter or other family members? If yes, why?

CHAPTER THIRTEEN

LOSS

Loss, the physical or spiritual death of someone close, like your mother, daughter, grandmother, aunt, or best friend is like having a limb cut from your body. I liken it to having a huge hole located in your body that you can't easily close. This chapter is for women who have lost significant women in their life. Twenty -four years before she passed, I was out of town when I dreamed that my mother had died and was lying on a large granite slab. Once I awakened, I called to talk to my mother, and she was very alive and well. However, since I was out of town, she did not tell me that I had lost my grandmother. Another huge loss!

Men and women have told me that there is nothing like losing your mother. In a theoretical sense, I agreed. However, it wasn't until my own mother died, that I felt the dramatic sense of loss that I did. I felt disoriented... lifeless... unable to make sense of my life when she died. When you lose your mother, you start to reminisce about your interactions with her. Did you do everything you could have done? What would you have done differently if you could do things over? Did you love her enough? Being an attentive daughter is challenging because you know if your mother needs you, you need to 'deal with her', be available to her, and yet life (at least mine) required a lot from me like raising children, working, being a wife, church and club member, etc. Life is like that. We always have something else to do when it comes to our family. However, your relationship with your mother is your link to your heritage and everything maternal. It is your connection with Mother Earth. So cherish your relationship with your mother, because there is none other like it.

I hate to admit this, but I took my mother for granted. I needed her, I loved her, but I always assumed that she would be here with me. While we had boundaries in our relationship, there wasn't anything that she wouldn't do for me or my family. That's what I will always remember about her. I am a harborer of secrets, but every now and then, I needed someone that I could talk to about those secrets, and it was usually my mother. She didn't gossip, she was protective, and sometimes overbearing, but I could rely on her. Once she passed away, I often found myself asking

God, to whom could I tell my innermost secrets? Of course, I shared them with God, but it was often a one way conversation—quite unlike that with my mother!

I was watching The Closer[14] the other night, and the main character, Brenda Lee Johnson, has been really worried about her dad, who had cancer of the thyroid and was recovering. Before she rushes out of the house to handle a police case, her mother asks if she could talk to her before she goes. She kisses her mom and tells her she will talk to her in the morning, but she has to leave. Once she gets home the next morning, she takes a cup of coffee into her mother's room, and says good morning... only, her mother doesn't answer. Brenda Lee goes to the side of the bed to awaken her mother and realizes that she has died. While the episode ends for the evening, I was left thinking about the times that I may have been too busy to stay for more conversation or to help my mother

---

[14] The Closer -
http://www.tntdrama.com/series/closer/?SR=the_closer_episodes

in some way. That feeling of regret does not feel good; nor is it healthy to carry.

For those of you who are close to your father, the loss of your mother is just as debilitating. I used to feel that my father understood me better than my mother because he was easier to talk to and not as quick to pass judgment. While that was true, I found that I could count on my mother to mean what she said. She followed through and was there when I needed her. As I mentioned earlier, my secrets stayed with her and she made sacrifices for me that I didn't learn about or understand until I began raising my own children.

How do you get past the feelings of sadness and disoriented loss? Older people used to say, "Just let it out." My advice is to pray and release your emotions through tears. Why am I advocating tears? According to Alternet,[15] "Emotional tears are elicited when a person's system shifts rapidly from sympathetic to

---

15

http://www.alternet.org/story/155447/why_we_cry%3A_the_fascinating_psychology_of_emotional_release parasympathetic activity—from a state of high tension to a period of recalibration and recovery." I believe crying is the soul's opportunity for cleansing. Just like laughter is good for the soul, crying is also. Shedding tears makes us feel better. [16]

According to a biblical passage in Luke, "Blessed are you who weep now, for you shall laugh," (Luke 6:21). Likewise, in Matthew 5:4, "Blessed are those who mourn, for they shall be comforted." [17]

My prayer was that I would be able to be whole again and not continue to mourn the loss of my mother for days at a time. I also prayed that I would be the kind of mother to my children that they needed me to be, just as my mother was to me and my siblings. How long did I mourn? It took a while before I could get through my days without crying. I think what I missed most was being able to pick up the phone and talk to her. I realized that her

---

[16] http://www.livescience.com/7854-theory-cry.html
[17] New King James version of the Bible

spirit was with me, but it didn't feel the same because I was so used to her being with me physically.

Initially, as we prepared her house for selling, everything I touched reminded me of her. That was really tough on my sister and I. It's funny, in our society people are comfortable mourning your losses with you as long as you don't 'carry on' too long. Yet, what is 'too long'? If you are still mourning the death of your mother, grandmother, sister, or daughter after a year, most people aren't as sympathetic. Don't let anyone make you feel bad about the time it takes to move past your grief. It took me at least three years before I could think of my mother without tearing up or being emotionally train wrecked. Having said that, there are still days when I hear a song that immediately brings tears to my eyes, and I say, "That's Mom's song!" If your mother was also your friend, then your grief is even more profound because you have not only lost your mother, you have lost a close friend.

Two years before my mother passed, I suffered the loss of my best friend from lung cancer. It was a more cerebral experience because she called me when she was first diagnosed with cancer, and we got to spend time together. I was so mad at her because she was a smoker, and even throughout her treatments, she continued to smoke. Unbelievable, right?! We were lucky enough to commune together for the next two years before she left this world. I thought of her often and grieved for quite a while after her death.

How do you handle the loss of a daughter? While I believe and say in my earlier books that children are a gift from God, once they are in your life, you can't ever imagine life without them. You should never have to bury your child, so when it happens the sense of loss is heightened. I have spoken to women who have lost their daughters, and the sense of disconnectedness is very much like losing a part of your body. I liken the feeling to losing an arm or leg. The pain is severe in the beginning, but with time you eventually adjust to the loss of that limb.

Eventually, you will wake up and discover that the sun is shining and that the gray fog that was hanging over you has lifted, at least for a moment. Each day that you feel the fog lift from your heart, thank God and hug the remaining members of your family.

STUDY GUIDE QUESTIONS FOR

LOSS:

1. Have you had any family losses (deaths)? If yes, explain the relationship you had with him/her.

2. Have you lost a significant female family member? Explain how you coped and how long it took for you to move past your grief.

3. In dealing with grief, what is your advice?

CHAPTER FOURTEEN

I'M SO PROUD OF YOU

According to life's evolutionary cycle, our daughters are born from us; we love, nurture, and raise them with our core values and customs, and then they grow up to make us proud mothers. This cycle continues as our princesses become queens, (marry) and have princesses and princes of their own, thus the positive cycle of regeneration occurs.

Just like a mighty oak develops from a single acorn, a young girl can birth an entire nation. Personally I am delighted to be a mother of two wonderful, educated, independent, and beautiful daughters who are making a positive impact in our world. But the road they traveled from young girl to woman was fraught with danger, distractions, and challenges. We tell our girls to get an education, travel, marry and have children. But that just might be our own idea of a successful life route. There are so many roads to take to get to the type of life that will make your daughter happy. Maybe she does not want to go to school; having children or getting married may not be in her dream chest. The fact that she made it to adulthood is a blessing from God. Being educated, employed, able to manage money *and* pay her bills puts her in the top 15% of the world's successful people. When I googled successful parenting of daughters, I got many references to Tiger Moms and Asian parenting, but not a lot of references to American standards. Don't American Moms have standards? Of course we do. Maybe successful parenting as a metric is not something that is being measured publicly. Depending on your culture, successful parenting of a daughter may be measured differently.

In some cultures, a successful daughter is one who has received a Masters' or PhD degree, and has a career. Another measure of success could be that your daughter is a stay-at-home mom and has raised a family. Maybe the way you raised your daughter led her to willingly serve others. Perhaps she was an obedient daughter and did what you told her to do. Or quite possibly you trained her to sacrifice herself for the sake of others. Any one or all of those could be attributes that you believe made parenting your daughter a successful journey. While there are many ways to measure your daughter's success, no matter how you measure it, be proud of your daughter.

Now, I've talked about this, but ask yourself this question… Are you *proud* of your daughter? I certainly am proud of mine. Let me tell you why. They're smart, are able to think on their feet, are discerning (they do not fall for the "okeydoke"), can problem solve, but are not afraid to ask for help if necessary, are ladies of strong faith, self-assured, self-respecting, and the list goes on. Those are just their internal attributes. They also interact well socially and go after what they want. The biggest reason that I'm proud is because they can take care of themselves. This is not to say that misfortune couldn't happen that causes them to have to move back home, or need to be supported emotionally, physically or mentally. But right now, they're strong and they're independent.

Also, did you notice that I said nothing about money or material things? To me, those things have nothing to do with the quality of their adult life. In addition, I didn't mention whether they were Rhodes Scholars with full scholarships or worked their way through school. It didn't – and doesn't matter. Both of my princesses did what was necessary to complete their education and begin their careers.

I started thinking about the times that I was most proud of my daughters. One time was when my daughter was a teenager and planning to attend a party. She discussed the pros and cons of attending "the party". It was being held at a local family center and we were talking about what to do if trouble occurred (fighting, underage drinking, etc.). Even though I planned to pick her up after the party, just having that discussion was problematic enough for her to decide it wasn't 'worth attending' the party. So she stayed home. *I was so surprised but very pleased and proud of her!*

I also remember my other daughter's senior year in college. She had decided to graduate and begin working. She didn't plan to attend graduate school. Personally I did not agree with her decision, but was willing to support what she decided to do. During her decision process, she ran into a couple of friends who had decided that completing their undergraduate degree was not enough to sustain them and they were planning to attend graduate school. Before the winter break was over, she too had decided to attend graduate school. *What a proud mama I was!* Not because of graduate school per se, but because of how she thought about and reconsidered her decision.

To me, being proud of your daughter means that you are thankful to God for seeing her grow into a wonderful woman. Is there ever a time when you are not proud of your daughter? Possibly. A daughter who runs out on her family, or is addicted to alcohol or drugs might be times when you are less proud of her. But before the disappointment sets in, is there anything else you can do to help her? What about women who have children and have no intention of marrying their child's father? I know in today's times, many young women are deciding to start their families without waiting until marriage. Being an old-fashioned woman, I think that road is pretty complicated and risky. I have always believed that children benefit from having both parents in their lives.

Single parenting is exhausting and in my humble opinion requires additional role models to replace the parent that is missing in the household. While I am pleased that my daughters have decided to wait until marriage to have children, had they chosen to become single parents, I wouldn't like it, but would support their decision and expect them to raise their children into awesome people. Did I just put my foot in my mouth? *Oh well!* Remember in Chapter One, I said chalk up my strong opinions to my current stage in life. I do believe God has a purpose for each of us. Sometimes the road that we travel, no matter how difficult, is necessary for our life's growth. So the young, single mother with four kids and no visible means of support may need the challenges that she is facing in order to be a stronger person. I have digressed a bit..

Mothers, tell your daughter (often) how important she is to you and how proud you are of her. Shower her with love, hugs, wonderful experiences, and honest conversation. Encourage her to be the best that she can be, because that will be how she responds to the people in her world. If you have to chastise her, do it

lovingly, infrequently and without judgment. Give her the best of

you, and you will have made a tremendous difference in this

world.

STUDY GUIDE QUESTIONS FOR

I'M SO PROUD OF YOU:

1. How comfortable are you telling your daughter you love her? Explain why you so comfortable or not so.

2. If you were gone and your daughter was being interviewed, what kind of relationship would she say the two of you had?

3. Does your daughter know you are proud of her? What have you have done to show your pride?

4. What barriers exist between you and your daughter that keep you from telling her that you love her?

CHAPTER FIFTEEN

CONCLUSION

This concluding chapter is a summary of reflections, memories, and anecdotes from just a few mothers and daughters that contacted me before I completed this third book in my series of parenting books. While this grouping is in no way complete, it is representative of the collective comments from women who mothered or were mothered in this journey called life.

I can remember when my oldest daughter had her first child. In my mind I said, "Boy are you getting ready to see all I tried to teach you now!" As time goes on, and as her daughter is getting older (trying her patience sometimes), I find myself encouraging her through all of the "I told you so (na-na-nie na-na)" times and forgetting about the trying times she put me through. It is more important that I encourage her to not make some of the same mistakes I made or what I did as a correction that was effective. It wasn't always easy. But, she has turned out to be an outstanding wife and mother. I can't help but stick my chest out, knowing that prayer and my family helped me mold her into awesomeness.

Sharon A.

৵৵৵৵৵৵৵৵৵৵৵৵৵৵৵

10 year old Taylor: Mom just got one question
Me: What?
Taylor: If this is your house, why am I the one always cleaning it?
Me: Hmm 5…4…3…2…
Taylor: Okay I'm leaving!!!!

Taleatha W.

🐦🐦🐦🐦🐦🐦🐦🐦🐦🐦🐦🐦🐦🐦🐦

Singing "the wheels on the bus go round and round, round and round" my five year old at the time stops and says "Mom!" Long pause, I knew I was in trouble then, as I glanced at her thru the review mirror. She was staring out the car window. She starts in with "I was thinking, why do the leaves fall off the trees?" Goodness, really she couldn't think of anything else to ask this Sunday morning! My explanation, "Well Luv, remember how the bears slept all winter, how God maintained them during the cold months. That's kind of what happens to the trees and flowers and grass. God put them on hold until it gets warm again." I was so proud of myself. Her response "Mom please don't get mad, but that sounds silly because trees don't have eyes"! She is still very literal to this day!
TC

🐦🐦🐦🐦🐦🐦🐦🐦🐦🐦🐦🐦🐦🐦🐦

When my daughter Zarinah was born, I consecrated her to the Lord. After all, she was His before mine. I looked at her 6 pound 5 oz. tiny but healthy body and thought how privileged I was to be her mommy. I promised God to teach her of Him, unconditionally love her, and listen to her with an open heart. And finally, discipline her when needed. My daughter is grown now with a husband and children of her own. She is smart, beautiful, witty and strong willed, and has a relationship with the Lord. Now married with children of her own, I reflect back to her birth. I realize nothing has changed except maybe the discipline, because she is not only my daughter, she is my friend.

Patti Ruth

১৯১৯১৯১৯১৯১৯১৯১৯১৯

One of my favorite memories with my only daughter Lauren is when she was about five years old. Lauren was learning to read. I am an avid reader too. We would climb up in my bed, lay back on the pillows and read Dr. Seuss books. I would read a part of a sentence and Lauren would chime in when she recognized a word or sentence. She often had memorized the whole book. One of our favorites was "Are You My Mother". And without fail at the end of this book, she would throw her arms around me, hug me tight and scream "You are My Mother!" I always felt happy and loved. Mirroring exactly the way I felt about her.

C. Stewart

১৯১৯১৯১৯১৯১৯১৯১৯১৯

Being a single mother is never a woman's dream, but life happens and some things are just out of our control. Every once in a while some women are blessed with the opportunity to have more for their child. I will never forget the day my daughter Sophia asked if she could call my husband (then we were just dating) daddy. She was only three and we were driving home…she simply asked "Mom can I call my dede, daddy". I was so taken aback by this, so I asked her why? She said he does everything the other kids at daycare tell me that their daddies do. He is my daddy." After years of trying to do it all myself and give her my all, I realized at that moment, every little girl needs a daddy. A mom can only offer so much, and God blessed my Angel with a great one.

Ashley M.

❧❧❧❧❧❧❧❧❧❧❧❧❧❧❧❧❧

Addison's "First Act". I remember when we were pregnant with our first child, we didn't want to know the sex of the baby so we waited to find out…although I was secretly hoping for a boy and the office pool was actually pretty well split (boy vs. girl). When I got to the hospital, the baby's heart rate kept dropping with each contraction so I had to have an emergency C-section. While lying on the operating table I heard the baby for the first time and while I was listening to the cry, I anxiously awaited to hear the first utterance of the gender. Then the doctor said "It's a girl" as he held her up over my insides that were completely exposed. And before I could lay my eyes on her, she urinated right there all in my insides. I knew then my daughter, Addison would be a pistol!

PMT

ઈઈઈઈઈઈઈઈઈઈઈઈઈઈ

The day my oldest daughter was born, her dad posted a photo of himself admiring her (and her admiring him) and captioned it "I can't believe I get to keep her!" A close friend of ours who has successfully raised two daughters of his own replied "Actually, you're only renting her." I didn't completely understand what he meant by this. After 1000s of art projects, countless trips to the doctor, dance parties in the kitchen, dried tears, princess band-aided boo boos, mommy-bug date nights, bedtime stories and I don't know how many other firsts later I finally understood more fully what he meant the day I sat in my car alone and crying having watched her walk into Kindergarten on her first day. I knew she'd be ok. She's smart, caring, curious, and loves to read and learn.

She told me once when I started a new position that I shouldn't be nervous and I should just smile and say hello and people would be my friend. Those were my words to her when she felt nervous about new situations. She's been paying attention. Children always pay attention. It's my job as a mom to model for my daughters how to be a woman. How to follow your passions no matter what they are as long as you're being true to yourself. How to show kindness to others even when they don't always deserve it. How to love yourself and not base the amount of love you deserve on what others tell you. I can't do these things for my daughters. I can teach, support, love, encourage and praise hoping that the base coat of self-esteem paint I am laying sticks long term. Then one day, she'll get her first backpack and set out on a path that I as a mother can't lay for her. I can't protect her forever no matter how much I want to. I can only drive by and say "I was once here" and hope I left her in better condition than when I held her for the first time.

Susan

๛๛๛๛๛๛๛๛๛๛๛๛๛

Daughters–

As the oldest of 3 and the only girl, I felt extremely blessed as God gave us a family of girls. As the last two are in their teens, they look up to their twenty-something sibling more and more. One of my fondest memories happened the summer, 15 year old Taylor embarked upon a 22 day adventure to the Australian continent.

As Taylor prepared to leave the nest for her first extended period of time, I truly enjoyed our periods of shopping; packing and the laughter we shared as I interjected last little mother tidbits to keep in mind on her journey. It was sheer joy to have such extended moments of bliss (no disagreements, no piercing stares…). I realized she was going to miss us as much as we were going to miss her, she was relishing the time with me, as much as I was basking in the moments with her. I'll never forget her non-verbal expression of love during those days.

Fast forward to departure day and airport commotion is non-stop between Taylor, parents, grandparents, best friend's family, new travel friends, good-bye kisses, last minutes waves and all of a sudden she's off! To wind down, we head to a family favorite restaurant – grandparents and youngest child Briana in tow. As we wait for our meal, Briana leans against dad and a couple of tears drop – Astonished and perplexed, we ask "What's wrong?" and as she struggles to stop the deluge now flowing, she quietly says "I'm going to miss Taylor". Yes, the pull at my heart was immediate – and definitely PRICELESS!

Taylor & Brianna's Mom

ત્જ ત્જ ત્જ ત્જ ત્જ ત્જ ત્જ ત્જ ત્જ ત્જ ત્જ ત્જ ત્જ ત્જ ત્જ

I had always said that I didn't want children. When I got married, I knew I needed to complete the circle of life by having a child. I prayed for a daughter so that I would only have to do it once. I loved Cesili dearly but the duties and time constraints of my job were causing me to lose her in her preteens and early teens to friends and boys. Since I was a teacher, I was able to make (somewhat illegal) arrangements for her transfer to my school. That was the best move I could have made. I was the play director and speech coach. We rode to school together, she got involved in my activities (I kind of pushed her), and then she got the theater/speech bug. We had that in common and we loved it. We laughed a lot and sang and danced. We got closer and closer. When she graduated from high school and went away to college, I was devastated, so one could only imagine how I felt when she decided to get her MFA in California and decided to stay to pursue her dream of being an actress. We miss each other all of time but we still talk every day and when we are together we still laugh a lot, sing and dance. I love her so much. She is my most precious gift and a true extension of me and my husband, her father.

DW

ત્જ ત્જ ત્જ ત્જ ત્જ ત્જ ત્જ ત્જ ત્જ ત્જ ત્જ ત્જ ત્જ ત્જ ત્જ

I remember as a very young girl, my mom began to teach me not to follow or not to lead but to just be myself. She taught me not to be afraid to stand alone and to stand by what I believe in. She once said to me "you don't do something because they're doing it".

Today I'm a strong woman who is not afraid of life's challenges, so I will not give up; I know the challenges are only obstacles that I need to go around. I found that these same challenges have made me even stronger. Each challenge I've met has prepared me for bigger things to come into my life.

Tracie T.

ॐॐॐॐॐॐॐॐॐॐॐॐॐॐॐॐ

My favorite memory was when I was 12 years old. It was Thanksgiving Day. My parents hosted dinner for our extended family and friends. It was a great day. When I went to bed that night, I noticed a letter on my pillow. My mother had written me a love note. She explained how proud she was of me and that she was honored to be my mom. She ended the letter by telling me that I was her best friend "on this Thanksgiving Day, I'm so grateful for you". I can't explain how that made me feel. I cried and was more committed to making her proud. I never forgot her words. It went a long way in building my confidence, my humility and my commitment to continue to make her proud of me.

Erin

ॐॐॐॐॐॐॐॐॐॐॐॐॐॐॐॐ

My mom passed away in September 2008, at the age of eighty. I admired her because of the strength she always displayed. She was a hard worker inside and outside of our home. Her greatest gift was being a giver. She helped and cared for people. She was a Christian and taught me Christian values which I maintain today. She encouraged me to make wise choices. In my younger years, I could talk to her about any and everything.

When my parents retired, they moved from Chicago to my mom's birth home in Batesville, Mississippi because she wanted to be near her mother. She, along with her sisters, cared for their aging mom. One thing my mom did not know how to do was rest. This took a toll on her health. She was a nurse at her church. One Sunday while attending church, my mom collapsed and had to be rushed to the hospital. She was alive but unresponsive. My dad and sister were with her at the hospital. I talked with my sister on the phone while she was at the hospital. She shared that she had been reading bible scriptures to my mom and praying. I had been praying also. I asked my sister to put the phone to my mom's ear. I could hear her breathing. It sounded like she was snoring. I began to tell her how much I loved and appreciated her. My sister and I hung up and I continued to pray for my mom. Just before my sister called me back to tell me that Mom was gone, God had given me such a peace in my heart. Even though I did not get a chance to see my mom, I got the opportunity to hear her breathing and was able to share with her my love for her. That was a special blessing!

Bernadette

∼∼∼∼∼∼∼∼∼∼∼∼∼∼∼∼

When I look back at my mother now, I can only hope and pray that I can be half the woman she ever was. My mother left her homeland (Spain) to join the life of an American military wife with limited English skills. She came to America barely speaking English, but willing to learn and do anything possible to make sure her family needs were meet. She faced much discrimination throughout the way. She never once let that stand in her way. She was determined to have her family succeed. She is still able to maintain her marriage through all these years, regardless of the language and cultural barriers. She was also able to successfully raised two college graduate daughters despite her struggles with learning the English amongst several other things. She always placed our needs before hers; she did not let things get in her way.

Cass

ᡒᡒᡒᡒᡒᡒᡒᡒᡒᡒᡒᡒᡒᡒᡒᡒ

My relationship with my mother is something that has evolved over the past 27 years. As a child, she was my provider, first teacher and primary caregiver. As a teenager she became my cheerleader and my biggest advocate. Looking back on my childhood, I feel like she instilled in me as many important lessons about life that she could. While I will say sometimes I had to learn on my own, my mother did the best job she could helping me become a woman. Now, as an adult she has become my greatest friend, confidante and supporter. I can say without any question, for the first 23 years of my life (until I graduated with my masters), every major decision she made was based around me. Once she asked my father what he felt was the best thing about her; he responded: you are a good mother. While I'm sure she wanted him to come up with something else, that didn't involve her parenting skills! I do feel like this was a great achievement. Everyone can't say they have done the best job at mothering. And while I may be biased, I do think she is the greatest mom.

Brittany

ৡৡৡৡৡৡৡৡৡৡৡৡৡৡৡ

It seems like it was just yesterday, that I was preparing my daughter to go away for college in New York. Her dream is to become an actress; she's a theatre major and New York is where she has always dreamt of going to college. She's a junior this year, and I couldn't be more proud of how she is doing and of who she has become. But even as I write this, my eyes are swelling up with tears, I can't seem to get a handle on myself when she leaves to go back or for that matter even thinking about her going back. I mean, she's a junior—I should be used to this by now, shouldn't I? I feel foolish, crying as I do, yet she's my baby girl and I miss her, sometimes even before she leaves, because it's for long periods of time.

This time, I knew I wouldn't be able to say goodbye long enough while dropping her off at the airport, so I said my goodbye at home. I began to cry and Dani said "why did you do that, now you won't be able to drive". I knew it was true, but I took one more hug and told her I loved her.

Jennie P

Encouraging thoughts to my daughters...

Get a good education.

You can overcome any obstacle in life if you believe in God and put him first in your life.

You have to decide what you want to be in life and then chart your goal and write out the steps that it will take for you to achieve your goal.

Life isn't easy, you have to earn the things you want in life.

Love of yourself and others is the plan that God wants us to learn.

Respect yourself and others will also respect you.

Along the path of life treat others the way that you want to be treated.

If you make mistakes, have the courage to own up to your mistakes and apologize.

With this journey we take in life, we will stumble and fall; when this happens, pick yourself up and start over. Remember all of us make mistakes. Some of us make mistakes and give up and some learn from their mistakes and eventually overcome all odds against them.

I will always love you unconditionally.

Mrs. B

I brought two wonderful little girls into this world. They are several years apart. I raised them both as my princesses. I am grateful to God that they gave me very little trouble during those important formative years. Now, my two princesses are all grown up. And, although I am proud of them at times, I am not sure I am pleased about some of the choices they have made in their lives. Sometimes, I feel like they are wicked queens. Do you ever feel like that?

IC

࿓࿓࿓࿓࿓࿓࿓࿓࿓࿓࿓࿓࿓࿓࿓

All my life, all I ever wanted was a loving relationship with my mother. I would go over my best friend's house when I was younger and wish we had what her and her mother had – a loving and understanding relationship. For the life of me, I can't understand why she doesn't like me. We look and act just alike. I remember when I was 15, she came home from work and said "I'm moving, what are you going to do?" I just cried my eyes out. How could a mother do that to her baby? That's why when I had my daughter 12 years ago, I promised her that I would always be here for her and (would) love her unconditionally. And I have.

CT

Help your daughter become the wonderful woman she was designed to be. The way you treat her will color and bless both *her* life and the *generations* she will impact.

ADDITIONAL RESOURCES

At the end of my presentations or workshops, participants often ask where they can go for more information about parenting, especially when they need assistance with deeper issues like mental illness, divorce, violent behaviors or adoption. I have included a list of resources which may be helpful to parents, psychologists, physicians or educators.

Resources for Parenting Girls

Simmons, R. *Odd Girl Out: the Hidden Culture of Aggression in Girls*. Mariner Books, 2002.

> Explains the motives behind "mean girls", and discusses the hidden culture of female bullying that takes place silently and painfully with girls and women.

Simmons, R. *The Curse of the Good Girl: Raising Authentic Girls with Courage and Confidence*. The Penguin Press, 2010.

> Book that fosters girls' assertiveness, resilience and integrity by stopping the idealizing of the "good girl" syndrome, unwittingly teaching girls to embrace a version of selfhood that curtails their power and potential.

Friday, N. *My Daughter/My Self: The Daughter's Search for Identity*. Dell Publishing, 1977.

> Explains the unique interactions between mothers and daughters. Candid self-disclosure and hundreds of interviews, Ms. Friday investigates a generational legacy and reveals the conflicting feelings of anger, hate, and love the daughters hold for their mothers–and why they so often "become" that mother themselves.

Depression in Adolescent and Teenage Girls.
http://www.medicinenet.com/script/main/art.asp?articlek
ey=23376

Mental Illness in Children.
http://www.medicinenet.com/mental_illness_in_children
/article.htm

Sexual Orientation and Gender Identity.
http://www.apa.org/topics/sexuality/orientation.aspx

Advocates for Youth – Comprehensive Sex Education.
http://www.advocatesforyouth.org/sex-education-home
http://www.mysistahs.org/

Diet & Weight Loss
http://www.helpguide.org/topics/weight_loss.htm

Eating Disorders - National Institute of Mental Health.
http://www.nimh.nih.gov/health/publications/eating-
disorders/index.shtml

Centers for Disease Control and Prevention.
Suicide Prevention -
http://www.cdc.gov/ViolencePrevention/suicide/index.html

Intimate Violence Prevention -
http://www.cdc.gov/violenceprevention/intimatepartnerviolen
ce/index.html

Clinical and Child Psychology. The Therapist Directory.
http://www.psychology.com/therapist/

Addictions.
http://www.apa.org/topics/addiction/index.aspx

CPSIA information can be obtained at www.ICGtesting.com
Printed in the USA
LVOW05s0242080114

368545LV00014B/226/P